CW00496019

APPETISING BITESIZE

Words Of Life 2

Bolaji Oyediran

Copyright 2020 © 2020 **Bolaji Oyediran**

This book or any portion thereof may not be reproduced or used in any manner whatsoever without the express permission of the publisher except in the use of brief quotations in a book review.

First edition published 2020

CONTENTS

PREFACE

How it all began. I always embrace the power and the revelation from His Word. When deep understanding of His Word was unveiled to me in the past I just sat on it and hid it in my heart. Soon I was convicted by the Holy spirit to start writing it down. Then once written, I started sharing when opportunities arose. I was prompted to share to a wider audience regularly so I started emailing , using social media to share. This led to devotional writing.

This is now Volume 2 of the appetising Word of Life. Volume 1 is so encouraging and reaching out in power. His Word going forth and not returning void.

ABOUT THE BOOK

This book is a bitesize Word of life, easy to digest and absorb daily devotional. In the beginning was the Word and the Word was with God. In Him is Life, light to mankind. It serves as part of your daily spiritual nutrition.

The best nutrition of your day is from His Word, it speaks and ministers life to your day.

All Words, in this book is breath by You. Your Word breaths abundance of life. Every reader receives life in abundance; overflow in all areas of life. Like a tree planted by the streams of water that sends its roots deep down to the water, causing it to flourish through all seasons, Your Words through this book will cause all to thirst for You more and more and be filled with abundance of Your life. Amen

Now to Him who is able to keep you from stumbling, And to present you faultless before the presence of His glory with exceeding joy, To God our Savior, Who alone is wise, Be glory and majesty, Dominion and power, Both now and forever. Jude 1:24-25. Amen.

DEDICATION

To God the Author and finisher of my faith. To God the Word the source of my being, the source of this book. I bow in awe of You Father.

A CHAMPION

66 A champion named Goliath, who was from Gath, came out of the Philistine camp. His height was six cubits and a span. He had a bronze helmet on his head and wore a coat of scale armor of bronze weighing five thousand shekels; on his legs he wore bronze greaves, and a bronze javelin was slung on his back. His spear shaft was like a weaver's rod, and its iron point weighed six hundred shekels. His shield bearer went ahead of him." 1 Samuel 17: 4-7 NIV

Goliath was a CHAMPION because of his physical strength and all his gadgets and men feared him.

We, the children of the most High are CHAMPIONS because we wear the armour of God.

"Therefore put on the full armor of God, so that when the day of evil comes, you may be able to stand your ground, and after you have done everything, to stand. Stand firm then, with the belt of truth buckled around your waist, with the breastplate of righteousness in place, and with your feet fitted with the readiness that comes from the

gospel of peace. In addition to all this, take up the shield of faith, with which you can extinguish all the flaming arrows of the evil one. Take the helmet of salvation and the sword of the Spirit, which is the word of God."
Ephesians 6:13-17 NIV

David depended on the armour of God and he defeated the CHAMPION of the world, Goliath.

"David said moreover, The Lord that delivered me out of the paw of the lion, and out of the paw of the bear, he will deliver me out of the hand of this Philistine."
1 Samuel 17:37 KJV

You are a CHAMPION, reign as one.

ACKNOWLEDGE THE YOUNGER GENERATION

Samuel lay down until morning and then opened the doors of the house of the Lord. He was afraid to tell Eli the vision, but Eli called him and said, "Samuel, my son." Samuel answered, "Here I am." "What was it he said to you?" Eli asked. "Do not hide it from me. May God deal with you, be it ever so severely, if you hide from me anything he told you." 1 Samuel 3:15-17 NIV

Eli acknowledged the call of God on Samuel. Eli approached Samuel to tell him the message from God.

Do you acknowledge the call and gifting on the younger ones? Do you ask them what they have to give/say? Do you give them opportunities?

Eli could have missed the message given to Samuel if he did not ask Samuel? Knowing that God has visited Samuel, Eli did not look down on Samuel as someone young, maybe too young for Him to be asking what God had to say. Eli saw Samuel beyond his age; he saw God's hands upon him.

Samuel was first of all afraid to speak out, but Eli encouraged him. It could be scary for the younger ones to speak out and pour out what God has given them; they need to be encouraged.

A FAR COUNTRY

A nd not many days after, the younger son gathered all together, journeyed to a far country, and there wasted his possessions with prodigal living. Luke 15:13 NKJV

The son stayed with the father for few days after taking his inheritance. Then he travelled to a far place away from the father.

When the son was far from home, he wasted his possession. Without the connection to the Father, he made wrong decisions.

When the son got his inheritance and was still with the Father even though for a short time he was restricted. His father was near, so his decision making was guided and had some boundaries. Then he decided to remove the boundaries and go far away.

He lost all connections and wasted his inheritance.

There are those this day that are breaking their connections with the Father; they have not gone far; they are still near although their connection is weak. We Pray they will reconnect and not go far away or suffer loss before reconnecting. Amen.

For those who have gone far, they will return; it is never too late. The Father is waiting and will restore you.

A TIMELY GOD

There is time for everything and a season for every activity under the heaven. Ecclesiastes 3:1.

Harvest time is the most rewarding time, but before harvest is the time of growth. The time between sowing and harvest is necessary, a period that needs to happen before harvest.

There are times when it seems that nothing is happening, the time between sowing and harvest.

"The flax and barley were destroyed since the barley was in the ear and the flax was in bloom. The wheat and spelt, however, were not destroyed because they ripen later" Exodus 9:31-32.

In the land of Egypt, the plague of hails destroyed plants that were in their harvest season. The wheat and spelt was spared because it was not its harvest season.

Your season is guarded by God, even though there might seem to be no harvest now, yet you and your harvest are being spared from loss. It might not be your harvest time now because you cannot manage the harvest and the storm together. It might ruin you. At the right season, you will harvest and you will be sustained.

AFTERCARE

Immediately He made His disciples get into the boat and go before Him to the other side, to Bethsaida, while He sent the multitude away. And when He had sent them away, He departed to the mountain to pray. Mark 6:45-46 NKJV

After Jesus fed the five thousand with the Word, He fed them with food too. Then He made sure they got away alright. Whilst Jesus was taking care of the crowd; He sent His disciples ahead in the boat, He gave them a headstart to their next destination. This also gave them a breathing space from the crowd.

Jesus then went to the mountain to pray before joining His disciples. What an example, Jesus was not just the Preacher but looked after His crowd and disciples. Jesus was the last to leave.

After Jesus finished His preaching, healing whatever He had to do, He stayed behind to make sure the crowd was safely dispersed. After we have done what we need to do, how quick are we to leave? Do we follow through/follow up on our assignment? Do we go beyond to show our care and love? Make every effort to provide aftercare.

ABILITY AND WILLINGNESS

He has given us all unique abilities and gifts. What He has given to you, are you willing to lay it down? Not until you are willing to step out to utilize it will you be equipped.

To build the tabernacle of the Lord in the time of Moses, "every skilled person to whom the Lord had given *ability and who was willing* to come and do the work. They received from Moses all the offering the Israelites had brought to carry out the work of constructing "Exodus 36:2-3.

Hence, for those who had being given the ability by God and were willing, they were equipped to carry out the building of the tabernacle. In fact, they were overflowing with materials that Moses instructed the Israelites "no more giving of material for there was enough."

Your given ability, are you willing to utilize it? When you are willing, provision will be made to equip you in all you need to contribute to the building of His Kingdom. Be willing and you will be equipped

ABANDONED BOAT

The fishermen left their boat and were washing their net; they had given up for the day as they had caught no fish.

Then Jesus got into the abandoned boat and used it. He told Simon, the owner of the boat to push it off a little from the land, and then Jesus sat down in it to teach the people.

When Jesus finished with the boat, He ordered Simon to return into the deep water where he had already been with no luck of catching any fish. Simon obeyed, he caught so many fishes that the net began to break. Simon was amazed; he then joined Jesus's team.

Are you in a situation that you are washing your net, you have left the boat and given up? Jesus needs the abandoned boat; he needs you to come back on board and follow His leadership. When Simon taught the boat was no longer of any use for the day, Jesus used it to teach. After He finished, He led Simon into the deep water where he caught so many fishes.

12

Do not shut the door and do not give up. Jesus can use that same thing for His purpose and revive the hopeless situation. Simon was so blessed that he left the boat altogether to follow Jesus.

ACCESS THE BOSS

Then she called to her husband, and said, "Please send me one of the young men and one of the donkeys, that I may run to the man of God and come back." II Kings 4:22 NKJV

The Shunammite's son died and she needed to reach out to the Man of God - Elisha. She was focused. She did not even tell her husband about her mission; she just told him where she was going. Her husband questioned why she was going at that time of the day.

Elisha sent a messenger to her before she got to him to ask of her welfare; her reply was, "it is well." She did not reveal her heart desire until she got to Elisha. On getting to him, he sent his messenger to go with her. The Shunnammite woman insisted on Elisha. She did not give room to distraction or wrong counsel that might have stopped her from getting to Elisha.

Princess A once asked her mum who was upstairs in the house for a drink. Her mum asked - why didn't you ask your Dad who is downstairs where the drinks are? She replied, you are the kitchen BOSS mummy.

Sometimes we beat around the bush, wasting time and energy when we need to approach the main source.

The Shunnammite's son was restored by Elisha.

Know your source, know the boss, know the one that holds the keys and access Him directly. He will answer you and meet your needs. AMEN

ALONE

You could be surrounded by people but still be alone. People could proclaim to share your vision, be supportive but still leave you by yourself at a very crucial time.

Jesus went with His followers to Gethsemane. He took Peter and the two sons of Zebedee. Jesus' heart was full of sorrow, to the point of death. He said to His disciples, "stay here and watch with me." Matthew 26:36-38 NCV

Three times Jesus went to His followers and found them asleep. He woke them up on all occasions but they still went back to sleep at a very crucial time when Jesus needed them to pray along with Him.

The followers were with Jesus physically; Jesus chose them (Peter and two sons of Zebedee); hence He trusted them to also be with Him in spirit (praying). The disciples slept and Jesus was left ALONE, Just Him with God.

May we not leave those who trust us to stand with them alone, and may we not be left alone. May we always be present in spirit and body.

AT CLOSE RANGE

We are blessed to be a blessing. We are born to grow and bear fruits.

When the world sees us from afar, do we look attractive? Are we welcoming? And when the world moves close to us, are they impressed or disappointed? Is the world able to take out fruits that will minister change and growth, fruits that will affect them for good?

At close range are we just a tree without fruits and we have nothing to give, nothing to impact others, an empty vessel. Where are your fruits?

"Seeing a fig tree by the road, Jesus went up to it but found nothing on it except leaves. Then He said to it, may you never bear fruit again." Matthew 21: 19 NIV

Jesus saw a fig tree from afar and approached it, hoping to find fruits for Him to eat. At close range, He found nothing, He was disappointed and He cursed the tree.

Children of God, do you look attractive from afar but at close range, nothing to find? No fruits to pass unto others.

Where is your love, joy, peace, forbearance, kindness, goodness, faithfulness, gentleness and self-control? At close range, what can we see?

ATTENTION NEEDED

Busy, busy, busy, there is always something to do, so many things over a limited period.

In the midst of your busy life, God is seeking your attention; He wants you to stop, step forward and step closer. As you step closer, He will instruct you in line with His purpose.

"Moses was busy tending the flock; the Lord appeared to him in flames of fire from within a bush. Moses saw this, then he went over." Exodus 3:1-3.

Moses stopped tending his flock at the sight of the burning bush and stepped towards God. Then when the Lord saw that he had gone over, God called him. Exodus 3:4.

God is trying to gain your attention; look around. God is at work with His glory and splendour; He is all-powerful, Almighty and sovereign. God's status alone is enough to grab your attention to fear Him and to want to dwell in His presence always.

Are you busy and is God calling you to step out of your

business and step towards Him? He wants to reveal His plan/purpose to you. He wants to work in you and through you.

Moses responded to God and stepped out of his flock-tending work into God's agenda.

BE AT PEACE DURING THE EIGHT DAYS

And after EIGHT DAYS His disciples were again inside, and Thomas with them. Jesus came, the doors being shut, and stood in the midst, and said, "Peace to you!" John 20:26 NKJV

Enjoy the eight days. Before Thomas saw Jesus, it was eight days from the time he heard the news from the other disciples that have seen Jesus. Prior to that, they were all wondering where Jesus was. Mary had already told them that she saw Jesus. Jesus Himself had said it before it happened that He will rise again.

Thomas had all this proof and he spent an additional eight days in disbelief and confusion when he should have been embracing the news and looking forward to seeing Jesus.

There is enough proof around you; His Word never fails. Whatever it is, He has done it in the past; He can do it again. He never fails. During your eight days(your waiting period), hold on to the testimonies all around, His

Words because on the eight day He stood in their midst and said peace to you. Peace to you now, during the eight days and on the eighth day. Christ has settled all things, be settled in Him, and your eyes will behold His beauty over all. Whilst waiting for the eighth day for the physical evidence, be at peace.

BE FRUITFUL IN EXILE

Exile is not a pleasant place to be. It is a place you might find yourself due to situations beyond your control.

Even though the exile season might not be pleasant, it could be a season that you need to go through in order to advance you to the next level/fulfil the will of the Father.

How can you turn the unpleasant exile season into a pleasant one? By reaching out. Jesus the night He was going to be betrayed, washed His disciples' feet. He took the focus off Himself; He reached out to His disciples instead of feeling sorry for Himself/doing nothing.

Jeremiah sent a letter to the exiles in Babylon, "increase in number there, do not decrease, and also seek the peace & prosperity of the city to which I have carried you into exile. Pray to the Lord for it, because if it prospers, you too will prosper" Jeremiah 29:6-7.

Even though they were in exile, they were encouraged to be positive and engage in positive actions that will produce positive results.

In your exile, engage in positive actions that will produce positive results. Joseph also did the same; in his exile season, he maintained sowing positive seeds. In return, he blessed the land and he was blessed.

BE HUNGRY AND PREVENT HUNGER

66 A satisfied soul loathes the honeycomb, But to a hungry soul every bitter thing is sweet." Proverbs 27:7NKJ.

Hunger makes you seek for food. Food strengthens and keeps you going.

To keep hunger at bay, you need to be disciplined and take regular meals. When very hungry, there is a high temptation for **unhealthy eating**.

You need to **feed** yourself **regularly** spiritually. Be well-fed and never be at a stage of desperate hunger. Yes, hunger daily for His manna and you will stay healthy and prevent hunger.

There is the danger of eating **anything,** eating **rubbish,** accepting **false doctrine** and **going astray** if you are complacent and get desperately hungry.

Keep safe, do not deny yourself of His daily manna. Be

hungry daily to be fed spiritually, so you don't get hungry & eat rubbish. **"When you are hungry, even something bitter tastes sweet"** Proverbs 27:7 ICB. Be hungry and prevent hunger.

BE IN CONTROL

Do not drown in your success. Be watchful and be in control.

Whilst enjoying the harvest of your labour, your success, be careful not to drown in it.

Always be in control, in control of your success and your harvest. Your hard work with God's help has yielded fruits. Let the fruits be a blessing.

Whilst celebrating the fruits, while enjoying the harvest, be watchful. Do not let your achievement or success rule you.

Noah was a man that feared God, God honoured his obedience and saved him and his household from the flood.

"Noah became a farmer and planted a vineyard. When he drank wine made from his grapes, he became drunk" Gen 9; 21-22.

There was no harm in drinking the wine, but he

overstepped the boundary; he became drunk. He gave control over to the wine, the minute he drank too much.

Do not overstep the boundary; enjoy your success, the fruit, but stay in control. Do not let your achievement and success control you. The source of your control should always remain sure (GOD).

BE ORGANIZED

But He said to them, "You give them something to eat." And they said, "We have no more than five loaves and two fish, unless we go and buy food for all these people." For there were about five thousand men. Then He said to His disciples, "MAKE THEM SIT DOWN IN GROUPS OF FIFTY ." And THEY DID SO, and made them all sit down. THEN HE TOOK the five loaves and the two fish, and looking up to heaven, He blessed and broke them, and gave them to the disciples to set before the multitude. Luke 9:13-16 NKJV

The crowd needed to be organized before they were fed. Jesus said to His disciples, sit them down in groups. Once they were organized into groups and Jesus was pleased with the arrangement, He took the loaves and fishes and blessed it. It multiplied and fed thousands, and there was overflow.

We don't know how long it took to organize the crowd; it could have been a very long time.

Are we in a crowdy situation, is our life crowdy/crowded?

Is God telling you the long process? Crowds could be challenging to organise. You get organised, declutter. What instructions is He giving you? Yes, you are hungry for whatever but before you can be fed you need to .... Once you have done that, sit back, and see heaven open unto you.

BE RESOURCEFUL

Elisha said, "Go around and ask all your neighbours for EMPTY JARS. Don't ask for just a few. 2 Kings 4:3 NIV

You are in need and there are resources all around you to help meet the need. In fact, the resources are there waiting for you to use.

The widow was in need and Elisha told her to go and collect/borrow empty vessels from her neighbours. She did not need to go into further debt by collecting vessels that will cost her. She needed to collect empty ones (not in use) from her neighbours, not from strangers.

The vessels collected were then filled with oil that met the widow's needs.

We need to be wise. When in need, are there resources around us that we can use without additional cost? Are you trying to sow seeds that are borrowed at a cost that makes matters worst by increasing your debt?

There may be situations that require you to sow costly

seeds but make sure you are wise. The widow collected empty vessels that cost her nothing; she just needed to go round & search.

Are you going into further debt to meet your need, borrowing beyond your means to meet a need?

Be resourceful; be wise. Do not increase your debts; make use of empty jars around you. May the Lord open our eyes to see the resources around us, may we not embark on costly resources when there are empty/free resources all around.

BE SEPARATED

The work of creation has been completed. In the beginning, there was the sky, the ground and the water. All of these were foundations on which other life sprung forth and dwelt. It was all formless and empty to start with. God then called out the waters to be separated, the ones above and the ones below. He called the ground to be separated from the water. He then proclaimed that they should be productive. Genesis 1:1-20NKJV

You are part of the vast and massive universal, but you're unique; you have a special role to play. You have a purpose. For the purpose to be fulfilled, you need to be separated, come out of your hiding, come out from the crowd. As you yield to his call and step out in faith, you will be productive. When the ground was separated, it started bearing fruit. The water was separated, and then it started producing and served as a habitat for the sea creatures.

Then the water, ground and sky were all working together, yielding and fulfilling God's purpose of creation, but first, each needed separation. Come out of your hiding, come out of the crowd, and let your purpose be identified. Separate, you have a purpose, be productive, and be fruitful.

BEAR THE BURDEN

He said to his father, "My head! My head!" His father told a servant, "CARRY HIM TO his mother." 2 Kings 4:19 NIV

The Shunammite's son became ill whilst with his father. The Father then sent him off to his mother. The son died in His mother's arm. She then turned to Elisha whom through she had her son. Elisha brought the son back to life.

Sometimes we act like the son's Father. When there was a problem with his son, he passed him to his mother. Shouldn't the burden be shared and dealt with together? When we face challenges, do we pass it on or do our part to see things through?

For example, our government/leaders might be struggling to tackle the economic situation. Do you sit back and leave the problem solving to them? There is always a part to play. Apart from praying, what practical input can you make? We all need to work together to take our Nation forward. Bear the burden; be practical, don't just leave it to the government. Also, in various aspects of life, when challenges arise, be proactive and be part of the solution.

BEFORE IT IS RIPE

Ripe enough for harvest. Fully equipped, fully functional, productive, and fully ready for the task. Are you mature enough for the task? Is it time for you to be harvested?

For a fruit to be ready for harvest it takes time. When ready, it will be obvious; the texture, colour and so on will tell. The season will also let you know if it is time for harvest.

The Lord is at work in you, His work is in progress, and you will be harvested at the appointed time. Joseph was given a dream; he will rule. It took time for the dream to be ripe and due for harvest. David was anointed king, but it took time for him to rule. For harvest, he had to wait for the appointed time.

"The vines in your fields will not drop their fruit before it is ripe says the Lord" Malachi 3:11.

Do not be hasty; wait on the Lord when your fruit is ripe, there will be a harvest. It is a process, abide in Him and

He will cause you to yield fruits in due season.

You might be led/called to something, but is it time to step out; are you ready for harvest?

BEYOND EXPECTATIONS

Now a man who was lame from birth was being carried to the temple gate called Beautiful,......... When he saw Peter and John about to enter, he asked them for money. Peter looked straight at him, as did John. Then Peter said, "Look at us!" So the man gave them his attention, EXPECTING to get SOMETHING from them. Acts 3:2-5 NIV

The world around us is in need. The people around us are in need. The people are asking for help that will solve their temporary needs, yet there is a greater need that is neglected.

The lame man at the city gate was asking people for money as he could not earn money due to him being lame. He was sitting around the temple where he could seek healing. His healing will take away the need to beg for money. Yet he was only asking for money, maybe because he didn't think he could be healed or he has tried seeking for healing so many times in the past and has not been healed.

Then Peter and John came and the Lame Man asked them for money. He was expecting to get something. Peter gave him SOMETHING BEYOND his expectations. In the name of Jesus, he was healed; he could walk and start earning money.

The world around us is in need, seeking temporary solutions, we have the answer. Jesus is the answer to all needs; He gives permanent solutions. We are in a position to GIVE BEYOND EXPECTED SOLUTIONS. Let us reach out.

BLEND IN

It is great to stand out because of the grace and power of God upon our life.

Due to the power of God in us, we often want to show off. We want to stand out in our physical appearance.

When the queen of England is anywhere, she will stand out. Her physical appearance stands out. Even if someone has never heard of her, they will be able to spot her in a crowd. Nothing is wrong with that.

But Jesus came, the son of God, the king of the world; He journeyed on earth humbly. When with His disciples/crowd, His physical appearance did not distinguish Him, but He blended in.

When it was time for Jesus to be arrested, there was a need for someone who knew Him to identify Him among His disciples; He was not obvious.

"Now the betrayer had arranged a signal with them. The one I kiss is the man" Mark 14:44.

The enemy had to work harder; Jesus did not make it easy for them by standing out by His physical status.

Sometimes we attract the enemy; we make their attack on us easy by showing off. Be humble in your appearance.

BROUGHT OUT AND CROWNED

Jehoiada and his sons brought out the king's son and put the crown on him; they presented him with a copy of the covenant and proclaimed him king. They anointed him and shouted, "Long live the king!"
2 Chronicles 23:11 NIV

We are a royal priesthood, Prince and princesses. We are born to reign with our Heavenly Father. We are on a journey, along the route are various challenges/ oppositions working against our mission, wanting to kill steal and destroy us.

Our Father keeps watch over us; He protects us.

The king's son had guards watching over him. There were those watching over the gate, the courtyard, the temple and around him. He was fully protected against all those who could capture him and prevent him from becoming the king.

Then when it was time to make him king, they

BROUGHT HIM OUT AND CROWNED HIM KING. The Lord is watching over you, protecting you against all oppositions. YOU WILL BE CROWNED to reign with Him; the enemy of destiny will not capture you. You are destined to REIGN, a royal priesthood.

To him who is able to keep you from stumbling and to present you before his glorious presence without fault and with great joy— to the only God our Saviour be glory, majesty, power and authority, through Jesus Christ our Lord, before all ages, now and forevermore! Amen.

Jude 1:24-25 NIV.

CAN NOT COMPARE

If the Lord kept a record of our sins, who could stand? Psalm 130:3

The Lord punishes the children for the sins of parents to the **THIRD AND FOURTH** generation of those **WHO HATE HIM**, but shows love/mercy to **THOUSAND** generations of **THOSE WHO LOVE HIM** and keeps His commandment. Exodus 20:4-6.

His anger lasts **A MOMENT** but His favour lasts **A LIFE TIME**. Psalm 30:5.

Our Father is so gracious, merciful and loving. The ratio of **GOD'S LOVE AND MERCY** is incomparable to the punishment of sins. For those who hate Him and sin against Him, He punishes to the **third to fourth** generation, but to those that love Him He shows His love/mercy to **thousand** generations. "For as high as the heavens are above the earth, so great is His love for those who fear Him. As far as the east is from the west so far has He removed our transgression from us" Psalm 103:11.

CAN OTHERS TRAVEL ON IT

66 The land they left behind was so desolate that no one travelled through it" Zechariah 7:14. NIV.

The people of Bethel messed up in their walk with God and they were scattered and left behind a desolate land.

The light of the world, reflecting Christ and the book the world reads; that is what we represent.

In your journey, what mark are you leaving? What example are you? Are you preparing His way?

A Farmer prepares the ground and then plants the seed. Preparation of the ground is very important; otherwise, the seed will not be planted. Hence the farmer works on the ground so that the seed would have a better chance of flourishing.

We are like farmers; we need to prepare the grounds, our work with God, our lifestyles, our actions/reaction are the grounds we need to work hard on. These grounds are seen by the outside world and should attract them to want to sow their lives as a seeds.

Examine your life, are you preparing grounds. Can others travel on the land you are passing through; is it desolate, dry and not attractive?

May I always leave grounds that will attract others to travel on.

CAN YOU SEE THE STAR

There are many stars in the sky, can you see **His Star?**

Some WISE MEN from the East saw **His Star** and **followed it**. Matthew 2:2.

When the Wise men saw the star, they were filled with joy. Matthew 2:10.

The star led them to where Jesus was; they bowed down and worshipped Him. They **opened** their **gifts** and **gave Jesus treasures.**

There is a star shinning trying to gain your attention, are you wise? Can you spot it? Among the other stars, the wise men spotted **the Star.**

The wise men spotted the **star and followed it.** The star led them to Jesus; they were filled with joy. They gave Jesus their gift and worshiped Him; what a powerful unique encounter.

My prayer is that you will BE WISE in every season, you

will SPOT THE STAR, you will FOLLOW it, you will WORSHIP it, GIVE TREASURE/YOUR GIFT to it. JESUS is the STAR and He brings you a powerful unique encounter and joy.

CHALLENGE THE CHALLENGERS

Most often, when accused or challenged, we are quick to respond. We cannot wait to defend in situations or circumstances. We often want to quickly put others right.

The best way sometimes is to stay calm. Do not respond instantly to every accusation or demand.

Let us learn from Jesus. The teachers of law and Pharisees were trying to trap Jesus and have a reason to accuse Him. They brought a woman caught in adultery and asked Jesus, "the law of Moses commanded us to stone such woman, what do you say?" John 8:5 NIV

Jesus bent down and started writing on the ground. He knew their intention, but He stayed calm and kept quiet. They kept at Him, and then He said "let any one of you who is without sin be the first throw a stone at her" John 8:7.

Then He continued writing and when He lifted His head

up, the woman was by herself. No one condemned her.

Jesus stayed calm; He responded to His challengers by challenging them. They failed. If you could just take time to be calm, letting the Holy Spirit work through you, your responses in challenging situations will challenge your challengers.

CITIZENSHIP

But when he had spent all, there arose a severe famine in that land, and he began to be in want. Then he went and joined himself to a citizen of that country, and he sent him into his fields to feed swine. Luke 15:14-15 NKJV

A son was far away from home. He had wasted his inheritance and was now in need. He had to join himself to another country to become a citizen. He had lost citizenship of his father's country because he was far away.

His citizenship of his father's land had no value where he was and he had to join the land he had now moved to, to gain access to their amenities. This new country offered him less. He realised that he traded for less, so he returned to his original country to restore the benefit of his citizenship.

A British passport would not earn you full benefits in an American environment; you would need a green card. No other place outside God offers you better. Do not go away from his presence. You are a citizen of the great

City of God. Do not trade it for anything else; it is not worth it. When you step out of God's boundaries, you remove His cover - your citizenship devalues

CLIMB BACK DOWN

Then he LED Jesus to Jerusalem and had Him stand on the pinnacle (highest point) of the temple, and said [mockingly] to Him, "If You are the Son of God, throw Yourself down from here; Luke 4:9 AMP

The devil led Jesus to the highest point of the temple and told Him to throw Himself down. Again, trying to order Jesus around. What if He threw Himself down, the angels would have saved Him but He would have followed the instructions of the devil, bowing under his leadership.

It does not matter the high heights you have been led to by evil intentions; you do not have to follow through. Climb back down from that height to level ground, do not throw yourself into it.

No matter how far you have journeyed to get to the high height, get back down to the level ground under God's leadership. It might take you longer to get back down; take God's route back down. Do not let it take the Angels to rescue you; even if you are rescued, there are consequences.

COMPLETE DELIVERANCE
WITH BLESSINGS

Your deliverance will be complete and accompanied with a bonus.

When the Israelites were eventually delivered and release from the hands of Pharaoh, their deliverance was complete. Pharaoh offered partial deliverance on many occasions." I will let you go to offer sacrifice to the Lord your God... but you must not go very far." Exodus 8:28 "Let only the men go and worship the Lord ..." Exodus 10:11.

By the time God had finished dealing with Pharaoh and his people, he drove them out completely. The Israelites found favour and were also given goods, silver, gold and much more by the Egyptians. Exodus 12:36

God is at work and by the time He finishes, there will be no holding back. Your deliverance will be complete and accompanied with treasures/blessings.

CONCLUDE

The word of God is a lamp unto our feet; it keeps us on the right path.

We have His word and we use it. But despite our knowledge of His word, we sometimes end up making our final decision outside His word. We make our conclusion outside it.

The serpent approached Eve and she replied him with the word of God, "we may eat fruit from the tree in the garden, but God did say, you must not eat fruit from the tree that is in the middle of the garden and you must not touch it or you will die." Genesis 3 :2-3.

Few minutes later, she took the fruit and ate it with the same mouth she used to declare God's word. Note she took the fruit; the serpent had no ability to force the fruit into her mouth, she took it. Only accept offers in line with God's Word.

Eve started with the word of God in her conversation with the serpent. Along the way, she dropped God's word; she made a conclusion outside God's word. Make sure His word is the centre of all your moves. Make sure you conclude with His word.

Let His word be the wind in your sail, the reason why you live, and the captain of your ship.

CONTINUED WITH ME

"I have compassion on the multitude, BECAUSE THEY HAVE NOW CONTINUED WITH ME three days and have nothing to eat. And if I send them away hungry to their own houses, THEY WILL FAINT on the way; for SOME of them have COME FROM AFAR ." Mark 8:2-3 NKJV

Jesus had compassion on the four thousand because they stayed(continued) with Him for three days. Some probably left after one day and some after two but this ones continued with Jesus. Jesus will not let them faint in their journey. The disciples said:

"How can one satisfy these people with bread here in the wilderness?" Mark 8:4 NKJV

In the wilderness with limited resources, He is never limited. He fed them to overflow—what a Mighty God we serve.

Continue with Him, in the wilderness, stay with Him. Be reassured He will not let you faint; He will meet your needs when there seems to be no way. He is the way, just stay with Him. The four thousand stayed with Jesus; some came from afar. There will be an overflow for you as you abide with Him, even in the wilderness. You have come a long way; you will not faint.

CROSS OVER

We are able to cross over, no barrier, Jesus bridged the gap.

In your journey, you need to cross over various things to be fulfilled and to be of use for Kingdom purpose.

Challenges will come, hardship will come, but Jesus stands for you at all times. You can cross over using Christ as your bridge.

To reach out and share the Good news you have received, you need to cross over barriers. Step out of your comfort zone, cross over to those in need, the homeless, the lost, alcoholics, poor, elderly & unbelievers.

Be approachable, be accessible to the outside world, and let the world reach you because of Christ the bridge. Let Christ in you close the gap. Be the bridge for men to see the light and be free.

You need to cross over to those in need and be accessible for them to cross over to you. Now is the time. Time will come when it will be impossible.

"And besides all this, between us and you a great chasm has been set in place, so that those who want to go from here to you cannot, nor can anyone cross over from there to us." Luke16:26. NIV

DIG AROUND TO MAKE THE CONNECTION

B ut he answered and said to him, 'Sir, let it alone this year also, until I DIG AROUND it and fertilize it. Luke 13:8 NKJV

To get to the unfruitful fig tree, access was made around the tree to fertilise it. The tree can then get the nutrient and hopefully grow. The keeper taught of an alternative route to feed the tree.

Connection can be made to make a positive or negative difference. The devil tried to access Job through his family, friends, his belongings – he lost so much. The devil tried to get him to deny God. All attempts did not work.

On a positive note, access could be made to reach out to many. Parents could be won to Christ through their children, and vice versa. A friend could be accessed to reach other friends. An act of kindness to a stranger could make an eternal connection.

We need to dig around to access fruitless grounds. We have works on our hands to do. God is counting on us.

DON'T CHASE HIM OUT

Matthews 8; 28-34 "….two men who had demons lived in the burial caves and were so dangerous that people could not use the road by those caves."

The evil men chased the people away; they were dangerous. The people could not move freely in their land.

Then Jesus came; the demon could not stand Him; they begged Jesus. "If you make us leave these men, please send us into that herd of pigs. Jesus then said, "GO," and the demons left the men and went into the pigs. The whole herd rushed down the hill into the lake and drowned.

This incident was very scary for the herdsmen; they ran away and shared what happened. The whole town went out to see Jesus and begged Him to leave their town.

The demons begged Jesus because they knew He is the Son of God and has the power to destroy them. The town begged Jesus because they were scared of His power. The town did not focus on what Jesus' power did; it got rid of the evil men that took over part of their town. He gave them back their town (freedom). But rather, they chased out Jesus who chased out their problem.

It might be difficult to comprehend Jesus (His ways & power), but He channels it to help us. Jesus is alive and here to chase out our problems, don't chase Him out, embrace Him.

DON'T KEEP OTHER'S INHERITANCE

Out of the part of the children of Judah was the inheritance of the children of Simeon. Jos 19:9 ASV

Out of what God has given you is something you need to give out to others. All is not just for you. You are blessed to be a blessing. You are part of God's big family. His family is in need all the time. The world is in need. You have something that you can give; love, time, resources, money, share the truth, ...

give, and it shall be given unto you; good measure, pressed down, shaken together, running over, shall they give into your bosom. For with what measure ye mete, it shall be measured to you again. Luke 6:38 ASV

You have something to give, do not keep it to yourself. You are accountable. Do not keep other people's inheritance. You are blessed; your source is eternal.

DO NOT BE DRAGGED DOWN

We are all part of the body. We have a role to play to work in unity and harmony to help other members of the body.

You that are strong should help those that are weak—lifting each other up at all times.

Help was given to Moses to keep his hands lifted in order to win the battle.

There are times when you are trying your best to lift another up, but instead of the individual being lifted, you are being dragged down. You are being dragged down while the other individual is not being lifted. What do you do?

Do you continue to risk your own life? Do you give up on them? What do you do?

Do not give up on them; do not put your life at risk. Seek help from above and from appropriate sources. Be supportive, be wise.

The ten wise virgins that had oil were not selfish toward the ten foolish virgins. The wise virgins were wise; they did not put their lives at risk. They helped the foolish virgin by giving them wise advice, which was for them to go and buy oil of their own that will last.

Do not be dragged down, stay focused, be watchful, be wise, know your limit. You are responsible for yourself first and then others. If they cannot be lifted, do not let them drag you down.

FILL THOSE EMPTY SPACES

Jesus said to the servants, "Fill the jars with water," so they filled them to the brim. Then he told them, "Now draw some out and take it to the master of the banquet." They did so, John 2:7-8 NIV

There was a need at hand; there were empty jars of wine at the Wedding, and the empty jars needed more wine in them.

Jesus was invited to intervene and He told the servants to fill the jars with water, and the water was then turned into wine.

There might be some empty spaces that you are looking up to God to fill with specific things. Meanwhile, God is telling you to fill those spaces with something totally out of place. His ways are not our ways and His thoughts, not ours. God works in ways least expected.

When you fill the space with what is required of you, when you step out in faith, He will turn around and meet your needs.

For instance, it might be that you are looking for a job, and the free time you have at present is required to help do some charity work. By filling your free time with charity work, doors for jobs clan be opened. Our God works wonders. Be prepared to fill those empty spaces as directed by Him and see your needs met beyond measure.

END OF AN ERA

Now when it was day, He departed and went into a deserted place. And the crowd sought Him and came to Him, and tried to keep Him from leaving them; Luke 4:42 NKJV

Everyone likes to keep good things to themselves. You are blessed to be a blessing.

The people of Galilee have been blessed by having Jesus with them. The blessings of Jesus were for everyone, not just them. They tried to stop Him from leaving.

It was time for Jesus to move on; He had served His era with them. We could sometimes be like this, trying to hold onto things that need to move on to fulfil further purpose elsewhere.

Sometimes people have served us well and their time is up; time to move to another assignment. For our selfish gain, we try to hold on. We try and find reasons. Is there anything wrong? There must be a reason why they want to leave; maybe something went wrong. Things do not

have to go wrong before it is time to move on. Do not
be selfish.

ENDURE INSULT

It is not all about you. There come times when you need to endure insult to gain positive results.

A Greek woman begged Jesus to drive the demon out of her daughter. Jesus answered her, it is not right to take the children's bread and toss it to the dogs. Mark 7:27.

Jesus compared the woman to a dog. But she did not take offense. She wanted her daughter to be healed and knew Jesus could do it. So it was not time to take offense or time to be angry. The woman answered Jesus," even the dogs under the table eat the children's crumbs." Mark 7:28. Jesus was impressed that the woman did not mind being compared to a dog as long as Jesus could heal her daughter. Jesus healed her.

Jesus endured a lot of insult for our sake. He endured to redeem us; He endured to reconcile us back to the Father. He was insulted so many times, but He kept His peace; He was not proud; on various occasions, He did not answer back.

There are times when you need to take insult to achieve a positive result.

ENEMIES AGENT

We are not ignorant of the enemy; he is like a roaring lion seeking whom to devour.

The enemy never gives up. He is using various external factors to entice us, leisure, money, physical things. If he fails, he will try other means to get to you. He will try and use other means, such as using people close to you to get to you.

The enemy tried to arrest/capture Jesus so many times but failed, apart from the fact that it was not His time to be captured, there was another factor.

The enemy needed someone on the inside, someone close to Jesus that will give them the connection. Judas filled in the gap, one of Jesus's disciples. He handed Jesus over to the accuser.

Are you with me, when the enemy cannot get you from the outside, he will seek instruments within. It can be your close friend, family, children or your church member.

The enemies tried to capture Samson, but they couldn't.

They used his wife to get at him, it worked and he was captured.

My prayer is that the enemy would not get us; neither would he get anyone close/connected to you. Our close bonds will not join the enemy's team to get to us.

FOOD FOR THE JOURNEY

He looked around and there by his head was some bread baked over hot coals, and a jar of water. He ATE AND DRANK AND THEN LAY DOWN again. The angel of the Lord came back a SECOND TIME and touched him and said, "GET UP AND EAT, FOR THE JOURNEY is too much for you." So he got up and ate and drank. Strengthened BY THAT FOOD, he TRAVELLED FORTY DAYS and forty nights until he reached Horeb, the mountain of God. 1 Kings 19:6-8 NIV

Eating and drinking for strength for the journey ahead, we need to be fed with His manna. We need His strength to sustain and empower us for the journey. In times of weariness, we need more of His strength.

Elijah was tired, scared and fell asleep. The angel woke him up the first time, and he ate and went back to sleep.

The angel came the second time to wake him again, "get up and eat for the journey. " Elijah did and his strength was renewed. He journeyed on that strength for 40 days.

It is time to get up and feed from Him. In times of great challenges, weariness, when scared or whatever, it is time to wake up and receive strength. Strength to rise and journey, not time to be fed and lay back down like Elijah did the first time. May we hear the awakening voice "GET UP AND EAT." When more strength is needed, may heaven keep supplying the food until we have enough strength to journey in power till we accomplish His purpose.

FRAGRANCE

Jesus was anointed by a woman. You would think that Jesus being who He is, will be anointed by a special ordained person such as a priest.

Jesus however, was anointed by a woman. The woman did not realise the significance of her act. But one thing she knew was that Jesus was worthy of the best, an expensive oil. She poured the oil on Jesus; this anointed Him and then she used her hair to wipe Him. She gave a costly expensive gift.

By anointing Jesus, she did not realise she was preparing Jesus for His burial; this needed to be done. After His death, when the women turned up at His tomb to anoint His body, He was risen. There was no need to anoint His body; this was already done before His death.

The fragrance of the oil filled the room. Those around also shared in the fragrance.

As you do and give your best to God, you may not realise the impact you are making or how you are fulfilling His divine purpose. As you anoint His purpose, the impact spreads beyond your immediate environment.

FREED BUT DID NOT FLEE

We are free, no longer in bondage. Whilst walking in freedom, be aware of your actions.

Your actions will either affect others positively, negatively or have no effect.

As children of God in freedom, our action and reaction should be one that has positive effects on others and our environment.

Paul & Silas were put in prison for standing for God. In prison, **they worshipped God while other prisoners were listening to them**. Act 16:25. Suddenly there was a violent earthquake and the prison doors opened and their chains were loosed. They were free, but they did not flee.

When the jailer saw the prison doors open, "he was about to kill himself," but Paul shouted, we are all here. Act 16:27-28.

The jailer was amazed that they did not run away, even though they had the chance to do so.

If Paul & Silas had fled, it would have caused a lot of havoc. The other prisoners would have fled also. The other prisoners could have been dangerous, although we do not know their crimes. They could be dangerous to their environment.

Paul & Silas were put in an inner cell, hence the maximum security. So one could say, prisoners put in such a place could be high risk.

The jailer could have killed himself if they fled. Paul & Silas did not flee when they were free; they ministered to the other prisoners and the jailer by their actions. The jailer then approached them for salvation; he and his household were saved.

How do you use your freedom, to your own advantage or to the advantage of others? You are free, but think about how your actions and reactions affect others.

FREED BUT DID NOT FLEE

We are free, no longer in bondage. Whilst walking in freedom, be aware of your actions.

Your actions will either affect others positively, negatively or have no effect.

As children of God in freedom, our action and reaction should be one that has positive effects on others and our environment.

Paul & Silas were put in prison for standing for God. In prison, they worshipped God while other prisoners were listening to them. Act 16:25. Suddenly there was a violent earthquake and the prison doors opened and their chains were loosed. They were free, but they did not flee.

When the jailer saw the prison doors open, "he was about to kill himself," but Paul shouted, we are all here. Act 16:27-28.

The jailer was amazed that they did not run away, even though they had the chance to do so.

If Paul & Silas had fled, it would have caused a lot of havoc. The other prisoners would have fled also. The other prisoners could have been dangerous, although we do not know their crimes. They could be dangerous to their environment.

Paul & Silas were put in an inner cell, hence the maximum security. So one could say, prisoners put in such a place could be high risk.

The jailer could have killed himself if they fled. Paul & Silas did not flee when they were free; they ministered to the other prisoners and the jailer by their actions. The jailer then approached them for salvation; he and his household were saved.

How do you use your freedom, to your own advantage or to the advantage of others? You are free, but think about how your actions and reactions affect others.

GET SOMEONE TO STAY

Then He said to them, "My soul is exceedingly sorrowful, even to death. STAY HERE and watch with Me." Matthew 26:38-NKJV

We thank God for the people around us; we thank God for the support network. Iron sharpens Iron. We are built to help one another; we are not an island. We are not built to live in isolation. Even Christ the King reached out for support from His three close disciples. Do not isolate yourself in your high position; seek support even from does looking up to you, those serving you.

The three disciples might have fallen asleep but yet they were there with Him. Jesus was not alone. Do not be alone in your time of distress.

Jesus said to the disciples STAY HERE and watch with me. I want to believe they did some watching before they fell asleep. They stood by Jesus, that counts although they did not pray enough.

Do not journey alone; get others to stay with you. You

will find strength. The Lord will uphold you and equip you in your journey in Jesus name.

GET TO JERUSALEM

Now after Jesus was born in Bethlehem of Judea in the days of Herod the king, behold, wise men from the East came to Jerusalem, saying, "Where is He who has been born King of the Jews? For we have seen His star in the East and have come to worship Him." Matthew 2:1-2 NKJV

The star appeared after Jesus was born. The star was an indication of Christ already birth.

When God the Father gives an instruction/sign, He has already birth it. It is already settled. All you need to do is follow the sign. The wise men followed the star to Jerusalem from the East. When they got to Jerusalem, the star then led them step by step to Jesus. Initially, all the wise men knew was that the star was from Jerusalem. Once they got to Jerusalem, detailed directions were unveiled. Get to Jerusalem, get to His place of birth of new things, detailed directions will follow.

Even when it seems far away, know that it is always already settled, it is already birthed. Follow the sign.

More details will unfold as you take the step of faith. He is faithful. AMEN

GENERATIONS
CONNECTIONS

We all belong to a generation and connected to the past and future. We inherit things as well as pass things on from generation to generation.

The action of Adam & Eve affected generations. The death of Christ on the cross is affecting generations. Through one man sin entered the world and through another man salvation.

The will of the Father from the beginning is for all generations to inherit life/freedom. By choosing Christ, you will break the generational link of the punishment of Adam & Eve's sin; we wear the righteousness of Christ.

"God is a jealous God, punishing the children for the sin of parents to the third generation of those **who hate me**, but showing love to the thousand generations of those **who love me** & keep my commandments" Exodus 20:5-6. Hence if you do not love God, you can inherit suffering/punishment that is not your fault, but for those who love God & keep God command, God will show His love & mercy.

Christ set us free; He finished it all on the cross. He paid for all punishment so that we do not have to. Are you suffering a generation curse/punishment? Love the Lord, hide under His shadow. Claim your victory, be free. Break the generational punishment by your love of God. Be free. "Whom the son set free is free indeed" John 8:36.

GOD WILL EQUIP YOU

The Promised Land was given to the Israelites. It was a land flowing with milk & honey and the people who lived there temporarily were powerful.

The Promised Land was a solid one and the people that lived there reflected that. Your dwelling place somehow reflects an aspect of who you are/your status; for example, wealthy people live in affluent areas.

Your promised gift might not reflect who you are at present, but it matches where God is taking you/who God has made you to be. It might take time to measure up, but you will measure up by His grace.

The Israelites saw themselves as grasshoppers (weak), unable to measure up to the residents living in their promised land. The Promised Land required strong, able people to care for it so that it measures up to God's promise. Weak people would not have been able to maintain God's standard. The Israelites with time, will be equipped to be strong enough to occupy the Promised Land. "Little by little I will drive them out before you, until you increased enough to take possession. Exodus 23:30. What all the Israelites needed to do is stand on God's promise.

What God has in store for you might seem huge, you might feel unequipped but God will equip you.

HAVE A BATH

To keep clean and fresh, we need to have a shower or bath.

Following your shower, in the course of the day, there are areas of your body that will require you to wash again. Such areas are the parts exposed to dirt or vigorous use, like your hands or even your feet if you reside in dusty areas.

We are cleansed and washed by the blood of the Lamb. Amen.

Jesus washed His disciple's feet. John13:5 He did not wash their whole body. One of His disciples wanted Jesus to wash more than his feet. But Jesus answered those who have had a bath need only to wash their feet, their whole body is clean. John13:10.

Jesus only needed to wash their feet because after the individual had a bath, their feet were exposed to dirt/dust, so needed attention.

You are saved once and for all; you are cleansed once and

for all. Yes, in your daily journey, you will be exposed to challenges and others (dirt), there will be areas of you that needs extra attention from God/Jesus. Jesus will give attention to that area that needs to be washed again. It should not be your whole being that needs attention again. Keep under His banner, your whole body is clean, and He will perfect that which needs perfection.

Jesus said, "though not every one of you is clean. John 13:10 referring to Judas who will betray Him.

Have a bath and stay clean, do not betray Him and He will perfect you; He will keep your feet clean.

KING'S PRIEST

One day, as He taught the people in the temple and preached the gospel, the chief priests and the scribes with the elders came up to Him, and said to Him, "Tell us, by what authority are You doing these things? Who is he who gave You this authority?" Luke 20:1-2 MEV

The Chief priests the teachers of law and the elders wanted to know by what authority Jesus was operating.

The Chief Priest is connected to the temple and ought to know Kingdom's business. But yet his title did not do him justice. He was on the same level as the elders and teachers of the law.

You bear His name, are you in tune with Him? Or are you with others wandering around asking questions when you should know and confidently stand up for the truth.

You are a child of God, let it be reflected in and through you.

But you are chosen people. You are the KING'S PRIESTS

. You are a holy nation. You are a nation that belongs to God alone. God chose you to tell about the wonderful things he has done. He called you out of darkness into his wonderful light. 1 Peter 2:9 ICB

IN A MOMENT

Then the devil, taking Him up on a high mountain, showed Him all the kingdoms of the world in a moment of time. Luke 4:5 NKJV

In an instant, the devil showed Jesus the whole Kingdom of the World, just like that.

Sometimes you can get carried away and enticed by false information. Not all that glitters is gold. There is a need to seek the foundation of the information before giving in to it. Do not be fooled. You will know the truth and be free of the lies of the enemy in such moments in Jesus' name. Amen

In a moment, Jesus was shown all kingdoms of the world and offered to take authority if He bows down. There was a catch, Jesus needed to bow down to the devil who does not even have authority over the kingdom of the earth. Yes, the devil is able to deceive those who fall for him, but he cannot make you do anything; you have the final say.

When there is an enticing offer on the table, take a step back and examine it. Make sure the source lines up with God. Do not be hasty. Be wise. May God guide you at that moment not to bow to any evil intentions.

IN HASTE

So it was, when the angels had gone away from them into heaven, that the shepherds said to one another, "Let us now go to Bethlehem and see this thing that has come to pass, which the Lord has made known to us." And they came WITH HASTE and found Mary and Joseph, and the Babe lying in a manger. Luke 2:15-16 NKJV

After the shepherds received the news of the birth of Jesus, they went in haste to search and they found Him.

There is news that requires quick action. There is a time for everything under the sun. We do not know how long Mary, Joseph and Jesus were in the stable. It was a temporary accommodation. When the Angels spoke to the shepherds, they were told where Jesus was at that present time—in the manger wrapped up. It was night time, yet the shepherds went in haste. What if they did not? Would they have found Jesus still in the stable or would they have had to search further because of the change in location?

I pray that we will all handle heavenly news with haste. We shall seek and find, in Jesus' name. Amen

INSTALL IT AT A YOUNG AGE

And his sister stood afar off, to know what would be done to him. Then the daughter of Pharaoh came down to bathe at the river. And her maidens walked along the riverside; and when she saw the ark among the reeds, she sent her maid to get it. Exodus 2:3-5 NKJV

When Miriam was five years old, her mum trusted her with her baby brother Moses. Miriam, prior to this time, must have been brought up to be responsible. It was not an overnight thing; Jochebed trusted Miriam as young as she was.

Miriam was competent and brave to approach Pharaoh's daughter when they found Moses.

We need to empower the younger generation, teach them to be responsible. Boldness and wisdom should be taught at a young age. Challenge them as young as possible. When put in challenging situations, what is deposited in them will help. In their journey, equip them to stand up and be confident.

We have roles to play to equip the young ones around us. They have roles to play in God's plans and purpose. Help build them, challenge them, make them responsible.

When you trust them with responsibilities, it lifts their spirit, it expands their confidence and they feel worthy. Speak wisdom and boldness into the younger generations. At a young age, may they play significant roles in the Kingdom's business in God's plans.

JOIN HIM IN THE HINDER PART

And he was in the hinder part of the ship, asleep on a pillow: and they awake him, and say unto him, Master, carest thou not that we perish? Mark 4:38 KJV

In the storm, Jesus was at peace, sleeping in the hinder part of the boat. The disciples did not join Him there to enjoy the peace while the storm was raging.

We know this storm is passing, but whilst it is still rounding up, there is a place of peace. The place is His hiding place. The disciples missed out. They embraced fear during the storm when they could have joined Jesus where He was.

Choose to join Christ in that hinder place. The storm did not affect Christ in the hinder part of the boat. Not that Christ did not feel the tossing of the boat but it did not affect Him. He was at peace and sleeping. Whilst calling upon God for this storm to end, be sure to be where Christ is, His secret hiding place. A place of peace and no fear.

LIMITED

And the king, when he heard these words, was greatly displeased with himself, and set his heart on Daniel to deliver him; and he labored till the going down of the sun to deliver him. So the king gave the command, and they brought Daniel and cast him into the den of lions. But the king spoke, saying to Daniel, "Your God, whom you serve continually, He will deliver you." Daniel 6:14, 16 NKJV

The king acknowledged his limitations and said to Daniel, may your God you serve continually save you. He could not go back on his own decree. It was out of his hands, but it is always in God's hands, never beyond His power to do or undo.

In ignorance, the king made a decree not knowing the end result. God turned the end result round to good; He saved Daniel from the Lion's den.

When the king of the world cannot save you; when he can not save himself from his own decree, who can? There is a King above all other kings that can overrule all decrees.

His name is Jesus, at His name every knee bows. Amen

LOCATED FOR THE GIFT YOU BEAR

Saying, Where is he that is born king of the Jews? for we have seen his star in the east, and are come to worship him. Matthew 2:2 KJVA

Jesus was born in the manger because of lack of room in the Inn.

There were stars shining over His birth place. It was not an ideal place, but it was not about the place but about who was in the place.

No matter where you are, once God favours you with awesome gifts, stars shine over it. The stars will attract wise men bearing precious gifts. The wise men will then share with others what a blessed person you are. It does not matter the state you are in now. It didn't matter where Mary was with Jesus, the wise men located them and they were honoured.

For you bear His gift, you will be located with honour. It does not matter where you are; what matters is His hands upon you.

LOOKING UP TO HEAVEN

Stephen (a man with great faith and full of the Holy Spirit), he was richly blessed by God who gave him the power to do great miracles and signs. Act 6:5, 8.

Some people were against him, but the Spirit was helping him to speak with wisdom and his words were so strong that they could not agree with him. Act 6:10

So they secretly urged some men to say bad things against him. They brought him to a meeting of the leaders. Stephen took the opportunity to speak the truth of the gospel. They heard it and became furious. Act 7:54 But Stephen was full of the Holy Spirit, **he looked up to heaven and saw the glory of God and Jesus standing at God's right side.**

They took him out of the city and stoned him to dead. Whilst they were throwing stones, Stephen prayed, "Lord Jesus receive my spirit and do not hold this sin against them." Act 6:59. Whilst Stephen was going through his ordeal; he was **empowered from above.** Nothing else mattered. He did not get angry because he was resented and was not making any progress with the leaders. **Instead, he looked up to heaven and there was Jesus; he was encouraged. He was able to pray for his persecutors.**

May we reach the point that nothing else matters, even when things are not in our favour, may we be at peace and look up to heaven for strength.

LOWLY

For He has regarded the LOWLY state of His maidservant; For behold, henceforth all generations will call me blessed. Luke 1:48 NKJV

Mary was appreciating God for choosing her to be the mother of Jesus. Mary was lowly. Lowly probably in status, ranking low in the society.

Lowly also relates to humility (in manner or spirit).

Mary was favoured by God and promoted from a lowly state to a state where all generations honoured her and called her blessed. In fact, Mary is unduly honoured in that some worship her "Hail Mary mother of Jesus" instead of God.

My prayer for you today is that as you are lowly (humble) in spirit, the Lord will favour you and all areas of low rank will be turned into areas of high rank. You will be lifted. Generations will call you blessed. You will not be turned into a god, but generations will worship God, seeing His favour upon you.

NOT CONTRACTED JUST WITNESSES

'For this reason a man shall LEAVE his father and mother and BE JOINED to his wife, and the two shall BECOME ONE flesh'; so then they are no longer two, but one flesh. Mark 10:7-8 NKJV

The journey of a husband and wife is meant to be a joint one - party of two. More than two participants become a crowd. A crowd becomes extra baggage.

Jesus spoke; if you want to follow me, leave your family. In other words, leave your mother, father, brother and sisters and follow him. He requires us to follow Him and Him alone not the crowd or any other.

The decision to leave and cling should be a once and for all—no going back. There is a lot of going backward and forward, creating weak links that is giving the liar access to our relationships.

The contract signed in your marriage is with your wife/husband in the presence of witnesses. Apart from the two, others are just witnesses; let the witnesses stay witnesses.

You confess Lord as your saviour surrounded by witnesses. Witnesses are not bound by your contract, hence don't make them part of your contract.

NOT JUST WISE BUT WISER

The season we are in requires us to be wiser. In the parable of the ten virgins, five were foolish and five were wise. The time came when all the virgins were weary and they fell asleep.

The foolish ran out of oil but the wise had extra for themselves but not in abundance to be able to give to others.

Joseph, in the land of Egypt, stored food in excess during the time of plenty. He prepared the land for the time of famine ahead. Not only did he store just for Egypt, but he stored more. He stored, not like the virgins who stored just for themselves, but he stored extra to the degree that provisions were made for other lands. He was not just wise but wiser.

We need to be wiser and ensure our storage overflows, so we are able to reach out to the world around us. Our surroundings are in need of us and what we can provide. Long and thirst for Him daily, be filled and BE WISER, NOT JUST WISE.

ONE OF THE BOATS

Then He got into one of the boats, which was Simon's, and asked him to put out a little from the land. ...... So they signaled to their partners in the other boat to come and help them. And they came and filled both the boats, so that they began to sink. Luke 5:3, 7 NKJV

It only took one. It took one person, Joseph, to feed Nations.

Fishermen from two boats had given up after no catch. Jesus came on the scene and He stepped into ONE of the boats. I wonder what the Fishermen from the other boats were wondering. Did they know who Jesus was? If not to start with after his teaching, they would have some idea. Then he ordered Simon who owned the boat, to launch it into the deep.

What was not accomplished all day through the fishermen's hard work was accomplished just like that. Much more was accomplished; there was an overflow. The other boats joined in to reap the harvest. It does not matter which boat you are in now, the first boat like Simon or the other boat that was empty to start with, the Lord will cause your boat to overflow. Look ahead; harvest season is approaching. That which seems empty now will overflow. The recovery of unyielding labour is on the way in Jesus' name. I pray the launching of all boats onshore, launch to the place of harvest.

OUT OF THEIR HIDINGS

And when He had come out of the boat, immediately there met Him out of the tombs a man with an unclean spirit, who had his dwelling among the tombs; and no one could bind him, not even with chains, When he saw Jesus from afar, he ran and worshiped Him. Mark 5:2-3, 6 NKJV

We are not ignorant of the enemies; we are also given authority. We also have His power dwelling in us. The enemy could be scary but we need to know that we have Authority and carry His power.

This man with the unclean spirit dwelled amongst the tomb. Jesus was passing by, and he came out of his tomb, cried out and bowed.

May His power be Mighty upon us that the unclean spirit will come out of their hiding, cry out and bow.

Sometimes your kids would just come and confess their wrongs doing without you asking. Yes, it could be guilty conscience as well as His spirit that you are carrying.

The unbelievers hold back swearing words because of your presence. You have it in you, and on a bigger scale, enemies will not be at ease at your presence; you are carriers of His power.

MARTHA

We have opened our heart to Christ, and He lives within us.

You could have someone live under your roof and yet you could still be strangers to each other. Hence you don't know them or have a relationship with them.

A tenant–landlord relationship could be rich or dry. Dry if all the landlord is interested in is the tenant paying rent and looking after the property. Rich if there is a relationship apart from just paying and taking care of the house.

Some of us Christians treat Jesus in our life like a tenant that needs to pay you and look after your interest, even though he is the owner of the house(you) to start with.

Martha opened her home to Jesus and then attended to the preparations that had to be made. Mary her sister on the other hand, sat at Jesus' feet and listened to Him. Then Martha needed help in her preparations, and so she asked Jesus to tell Mary to help her.

Of course, Jesus was aware of the things that needed doing,

but those things could wait. Jesus called out to Martha, "Martha you are worried and upset about many things but few things are needed or indeed only one. Mary has chosen what is better."

We give many things our undivided attention and do not attend to Jesus. Then when we are struggling, we approach Him for help. To start with, your attention should have been with Him. Seek first the Kingdom of God and His righteousness and all other things will be added unto you

Sometimes we claim to be busy for Jesus but yet we neglect time with Him as well. Jesus was busy going around doing God's business but He always withdrew to be alone with God.

MEANT FOR EVIL

All things work out for good for those who love Him and are called according to His purpose. But God has chosen the foolish things of the world to put to shame the wise, and God has chosen the weak things of the world to put to shame the things which are mighty. I Corinthians 1:27 NKJV

The enemies who put Jesus to death thought they won; little did they know that they helped fulfill God's plan. The process was painful for Christ of course, but the pain suffered cannot be compared to the significance of His death. His death paid the price of our shortcomings, brought redemption and life in abundance.

It is working out for good those challenges and trials. Your life is secure in Him; His plan and purposes are good. The process of His goodness might not be pleasant but the best place to be is in the center of His plans. He will sustain you through it and the end result brings total recovery and much more.

That dark place is bringing forth power. The enemies

might think they are winning but they are helping to fulfil the plan of God. God is in control. Amen.

PAYS THE RIGHT WAGES

And about the eleventh hour he went out and found others standing idle, and said to them, 'Why have you been standing here idle all day?' They said to him, 'Because no one hired us.' He said to them, 'You also go into the vineyard, and whatever is RIGHT YOU WILL RECEIVE.' Matthew 20:6-7 NKJV

The landowner hired labourers at different hours of the day up to the eleventh hour. They all got paid the same wages. Those who were there first were not pleased.

At the start of hiring, the wages for the day was set at one denarius. As the hours went by and more labourers were hired, the landowners promised to pay WHAT IS RIGHT.

All the labourers that positioned themselves for a job got THE RIGHT WAGES.

There is enough room and resources with the Father. It does not matter what time you show up—First hour, eleventh hour. In His vineyard, there is provision for everyone, no time limit. It is never too late. It is not over till it is over.

It doesn't matter if some call you a latecomer, the landowner (Father) has your back covered.

It does not matter if it is the morning, afternoon or evening season of your life, reach out to the landowner. He pays the right wages and has room for you, and for everyone.

PERSECUTED, SCATTERED AND FOCUSED

Wherever you are, regardless of how you got there, be focused.

We often blame our present circumstances on something that happened in the past, especially if we are not where we planned to be.

Negative and positive situations reposition us. When you are repositioned due to whatever reason, are you maintaining your focus and purpose?

As a child of God, He should be your focus. As far as you make Him your source at all times, you are a winner. "Everything works out for good for those who love God and are called according to His purpose." Romans 8:28

"A great persecution broke out against the church in Jerusalem **and all** except the apostle **were scattered**." Act 8:1. Hence many were scattered and repositioned. "Those who had been scattered preached the word wherever they went." Acts 8:4.NIV. Those who were scattered stayed focused, their purpose was not scattered; they continued their purpose, reached out to a new territory," so there was great joy in that city." Acts 8:8.

Situation, circumstance negative/positive might place you where you did not intend, but it should not change your purpose. You are in control, stay focused. Wherever you might be, regardless of how you got there, be focused on your God's given purpose.

REGISTER

So all went to be REGISTERED EVERYONE TO HIS OWN CITY. Joseph also went up from Galilee, ... to be registered with Mary, his betrothed wife, who was with child. So it was, that while they were there, the days were completed for her to be delivered. Luke 2:3-6 NKJV.

It was time to register and Joseph and Mary went to Bethlehem. Mary was heavily pregnant, yet she was not exempt from the journey.

Everyone needed to go to their source, their home town to be registered, their place of birth.

Where do we come from, who birthed us?

'And in the beginning, God made man in His likeness,' - our birth place originates from our Heavenly Father.

There is a call for the whole world to register with our source, the source of our being. We need to register our name in His book.

No matter how challenging it could be, as it was for Mary who was heavily pregnant, you need to make the journey.

No matter what stage you are in your journey, you might be experiencing pleasant or unpleasant times, no exemption, all are required to come as they are.

You need to make the journey to the foot of the cross where access is made to the book of life where your name needs to be.

Joseph went up with Mary. I pray that we and our household will be registered; no one will be left out.

REJECTED BUT FOCUSED

Then Jesus returned in the power of the Spirit to Galilee, and news of Him went out through all the surrounding region. And He taught in their synagogues, being glorified by all. Luke 4:14-15 NKJV

Following Jesus ordeal in the wilderness He returned with power to Galilee, many were drawn to Him.

Then He went to Nazareth where He was brought up. He was rejected there. You would think He would get more support from where He was well known. Sometimes we are rejected by our very own.

So all those in the synagogue, when they heard these things, were filled with wrath, and rose up and thrust Him out of the city; and they led Him to the brow of the hill on which their city was built, that they might throw Him down over the cliff. Luke 4:28-29 NKJV

No matter how filled and powerful you are in Him, be prepared to be rejected and fought against.

Jesus was able and moved on; in fact, He passed through

the very crowd that were trying to harm Him untouched.

Jesus kept making impact and reaching many. He stayed focused. Keep focus during rejection and move on.

SERVANT

Our Lord, our example, He came to serve and not to be served. Abraham was required by God to sacrifice his only son. On the way to make the sacrifice, "he took with him two of his **servants** and his son Isaac" Genesis 22:3.

On the third day of their journey Abraham looked up and saw the place in the distance. He said to his servants, "stay here with the donkey while I and the boy go over there. We will worship and then we will come back to you." Genesis 22:4-5.

Abraham took two servants with him; they had a role to play. Their role was for the journey, so when Abraham saw his destination, he ordered the servants to stay put. The servant's role would have involved something like helping with the carrying of the wood, serving as a company for Abraham and his son.

The servant might have loved to be present at the sacrifice, but it was not their place to be. If present at the sacrifice, they might have been a hindrance as they might

128

try to stop Abraham from attempting to sacrifice his son. During the journey, the servant served a purpose but not for the sacrifice.

As servants of the Living God, we have a role. Our service might be restricted to an area, for if we go further, we might not see/understand God's intention. God might be saying, stay here; I will be back to instruct you of your next role for the journey. Have a serving heart.

SOMEONE CRIED

66 At midnight SOMEONE CRIED OUT, 'The bridegroom is coming! Come and meet him!' Then all the girls woke up and got their lamps ready. Matthew 25:6-7 ICB

At midnight in the dark, someone was aware of the coming of the bridegroom and cried out. What if this someone did not cry out? Would the virgins have woken up? We are the cry of our world today. The cry woke up the virgins, both wise and foolish and they got their lamps ready.

May we be aware of His coming, even in the dark seasons when people are sleeping, may we be aware and cry out to wake others up. May our cry wake those around us up just as both the wise and foolish virgins woke up. May our cry in the dark seasons and in all seasons wake up all, both the wise and foolish.

May all the woken up virgins meet the Bridegroom—may the voices that cry out also meet the Bridegroom.

SO THAT YOU WILL PAY NO ATTENTION

The devil is a roaring lion, always seeking whom he may devour. He never rests; he knows his power and time is limited.

We often fall short with time management. The enemy will try and fill our time with all sorts of things so that we have less time to attend to God.

The victory of the Israelites was at hand. Moses was sent to Pharaoh to tell him to let them go to worship God. The first thing Pharaoh did was to increase their workload, make it harder for them to achieve. His intention was so they will not be able to pay attention to God "Make the work harder for the people so that they keep working and pay no attention to lies," meaning to God. Exodus 5:9. NIV

Is work being created for us or are we creating more work for ourselves causing us to pay less attention to God?

"Remember the Lord your God it is He who gives you

the ability to produce wealth." Deuteronomy 8:18. NIV

Take control of your time, if struggling, lay it before God; it is time to give Him more attention.

STAND OUT

Jochebed was one of the so many women that gave birth during the death decree of the king. The other women most likely did not put up a fight. They gave in, and their children were killed.

We are individually uniquely made. There come times that we need to stand out and be indifferent when everyone is bowing under the obvious. You do not need to follow the crowd. Hold strongly to what God (Holy Spirit) is telling you. Hide under the conviction of the spirit.

I believe Jochebed did not broadcast her decision to hide Moses to everyone as that could have spoilt her action in many ways. She could be discouraged by others not to go ahead with such actions and they could have reported her to the enemies. There is evil on the heart of man; you can not be sure of who is for you or against you. If God is with you in your decision, you still need to apply wisdom.

So many share their vision prematurely. Joseph shared his dream and this caused his journey to be more challenging. It all worked out in the end, but perhaps his journey would have been smoother.

Jochebed was in a situation like others but chose to act wisely, depending on God. The fear of man did not cloud her vision. She took risks that paid off. Amen

STIRRING

When Jesus entered Jerusalem, the WHOLE CITY WAS STIRRED and asked, "Who is this?" Matthew 21:10 NIV

The entrance of Jesus into Jerusalem caused a STIRRING. The WHOLE CITY WAS STIRRED and they MADE ENQUIRY ABOUT JESUS.

The entry of Jesus was accompanied by power. The presence of God ministers to needs.

We ask, seek and knock; Father let your presence stir up the whole world. Let the world enquire of you. Let the world come to you and acknowledge you as Lord.

You then entered the temple and drove out the contaminant of the temple. Cleanse our world and drive out all contaminants. Your blood cleanses. Have Your rightful place. You taught and healed the sick in the temple. Let there be healing; let your truth be known and embraced.

Your Kingdom come, Your will be done.

STOP THE TRAFFIC

And He WOULD NOT PERMIT anyone TO CARRY merchandise or household wares THROUGH THE TEMPLE [grounds, using the temple area irreverently as a shortcut]. He began to teach and say to them, "Is it not written, 'My house shall be called a house of prayer for all the nations'? But you have made it a robbers' den." Mark 11:16-17 AMP

Not only did Jesus chase out the thieves and sellers, he did not permit merchandise to pass through the temple. Some were using the temple as shortcuts and using it like a common ground. They were passing through the temple without having any business with the temple; they had no regards— showing no respect- taking advantage.

We are His temple; we sometimes allow things to pass through. These things create traffics that contaminant our lives.

Those passing through the temple would somehow leave something behind their footprints, dirt, whatever.

We allow things that we think does not matter, things that seem harmless but yet are not—they have no business with the temple and cause contamination.

May our eyes be opened to stop the flow of unnecessary damaging traffic in our lives, in His temple, in His Church.

THE DAYS WERE COMPLETE

And she brought forth her firstborn Son, and wrapped Him in swaddling cloths, and laid Him in a manger, because there was no room for them in the inn. Luke 2:7 NKJV

So it was, that while they were there, the DAYS WERE COMPLETED for her to be delivered. Luke 2:6 NKJV

It was time for Mary to bring forth the Child that had been growing inside her; the days were complete. There was no room in the Inn; the city of Bethlehem was in chaos; we are not sure if Mary herself was ready. Regardless of the situation, the lack of room or readiness could not stop the birth.

There is something growing inside you, something great. The days of birth is at hand. In the midst of chaos, the days of completion is at hand, the day for it to come forth. It is out of your control; it is coming, be ready to embrace it. When the time of the birth is due, the child will come no matter what.

The day for you to bring forth is at hand and absolutely nothing will stop it, embrace the birth of something awesome in Jesus' name. The chaos around cannot hold back what God brings forth.

THE SEAL BROKEN AND THE STONE ROLLED AWAY

The tomb where Jesus laid was made secure as they knew how. "So they went and made the tomb secure by putting a seal on the stone and posting guard" Matthew 27:65 NIV

The aim was to try and prevent God's plan. Even though Jesus was dead, they were trying to stop God's plan of Jesus rising again. There was a violent earthquake from heaven that caused the seal to the tomb to be broken and the stone rolled away with the Angel sitting on the stone.

God made our heart, a heart of flesh (tender). Our heart connects us to the Father. Negatives forces sneak in and form a stone around the heart of man, blocking access and preventing God's purpose.

God is able to cause an earthquake that will break the seal to the stony heart and enable access to God. His plan will then be fulfilled. The seal to the tomb was broken and God's plan was fulfilled. May the seal to the stony heart be broken, the stone rolled away and God's will be established in the heart of man. AMEN

THEIR REPORT WILL CHANGE

It might feel like a curse or vengeance to people around you or to yourself in the midst of negative circumstances.

The world sometimes finds it difficult to react to negative circumstances. They will try and find a reason for it; they might say it is because of hidden sin; it is a curse/vengeance.

Acts 28:1-6 "After Paul's shipwreck, they were trying to get some warmth. There came another attack from the viper" The people reacted by saying Paul is a murderer, and is being punished.

Paul was saved from the shipwreck and the viper's poison. The report of the people on the Island now changed, "Paul is a god." Paul found favour and he healed their sick.

In the midst of all the challenges, Paul came to no harm, then the people's report changed from negative to positive. Those who were scared of Paul before, saying he is cursed and evil, came to be prayed for by him.

Whatever the challenges God can handle it, stay put. You will walk in victory and the same people who turned their backs on you will turn around and seek your help. THEIR REPORT WILL CHANGE.

TIME TO LET GO

There is a time for everything and season for every activity under heaven.

You may be currently engaged in that which is fruitful and bringing back good returns, but it might just be for a limited time. The time comes when you will need to let it go. When it is time to let go, it might lead to total loss if you insist and carry it on.

The Egyptians profited many years from the Israelites slavery, but their time of profit was up. Pharaoh tried to hold on to the Israelites; despite the plagues the Egyptians suffered, but in the end, he released them.

Then Pharaoh changed his mind and pursued them with all his horses and chariots, horsemen and troops. He gave it his best shot to try and gain them back. **In their pursuit they all died** in the sea and no one survived.

Yes, the Egyptians were Israelites enemy, but the Israelites were very resourceful. We are sometimes like the EGYPTIANS REFUSING TO LET GO OF AN

ERA. It has been resourceful, but the time is up, time to move on. We still put our all into whatever it is and it might result in total loss. Be sensitive to His guidance; do not lean on your own understanding. Do not let it all end in loss. Know when to move on; when you do, new doors will open. Know when it is time to let go.

TO SEE THE OUTCOME

But Peter FOLLOWED HIM AT A DISTANCE AS FAR as the courtyard of the [elegant home of the Jewish] high priest, and went inside, and sat with the guards TO SEE THE OUTCOME. Matthew 26:58 AMP

Peter followed AT A DISTANCE to see the outcome of Jesus' arrest. Yes, the immediate outcome was not pleasant, yet the end outcome paid for our sin, giving redemption.

Are you following Him close enough for you to see beyond the immediate suffering that will be conquered, that is already conquered? Or are you following at afar distance because of the fear of the immediate suffering/ challenges that would last only but for a moment as there is joy and victory beyond?

The outcome of the immediate challenges and suffering will end well when you draw close to Him. He has overcome, so we will overcome when close to Him. When you follow at afar distance, you will be close to the opposition. Peter followed at a far distance and became close to Jesus' enemies, camping with them and unable to stand for Jesus.

To see the outcome, how are you following Him?

Be sure not to be far from Him no matter what, He is the stronghold of your being. The best secured place to be when the going gets tough is to be close to Him; He will sustain you.

TO WHOM MORE IS GIVEN MORE IS EXPECTED

Then Jesus came with them to a place called Gethsemane, and said to the disciples, "SIT HERE WHILE I GO AND PRAY OVER THERE " And HE TOOK WITH HIM PETER AND THE TWO SONS of Zebedee, and He began to be sorrowful and deeply distressed. Then He said to them, "My soul is exceedingly sorrowful, even to death. STAY HERE AND WATCH WITH ME ." He WENT A LITTLE FARTHER and fell on His face, AND PRAYED, saying.... " Matthew 26:36-39 NKJV

Gethsemane had three areas to it. First, the sit here whilst I go and pray area. Secondly, the stay here and pray with me area and thirdly the stay awake praying alone area.

Jesus said to some, sit here while I go and pray over there. Then He took three of them with Him further into Gethsemane and said to this group, stay here and pray with me. He went farther more Himself to pray.

Jesus did not instruct the first group to pray; He just told them to sit. He took the second group of three further and told them to stay and pray. More was expected from this group. He revealed to them His deep feelings of sorrow and distress. They fell asleep instead of praying.

To whom more is given, more is expected. When we draw close to Him, He draws close to us. When more is revealed to us, more is expected. Sometimes we want the deep things of the spirit to be revealed to us, but we do not want the responsibility that comes with it. We want to be close to God but don't want the responsibility.

For the disciples in the first area of Gethsemane, Jesus did not even tell them to pray and He did not tell them His feelings. His heart was not revealed to them. They were not condemned for sleeping, for there was no expectation from them.

As we draw close and more is revealed, may we stand up to the responsibility.

WHERE MY PEOPLE LIVE

We are His seeds scattered all over the universe. We should influence our surroundings for good.

For the sake of the righteous in Sodom/Gomorrah, God was prepared to have mercy on the Land. "What if only ten can be found there? God answered for the sake of ten I will not destroy it," Genesis 18:32.

We are where we are to bring a change for the better, to shed light in dark places. For your sake, things can be turned around for better.

Know who you are in Christ Jesus, use your influence in Christ to rescue your surroundings, your Land. "I will deal differently with the land of Goshen, where my people live" Exodus 8:22. Because you dwell in that land, ask God for breakthrough/victory. Ask and keep asking till victory is won. In the case of Abraham pleading for the Land of Sodom and Gomorrah, he stopped asking when he reached ten righteous people. Who knows if he kept asking for fewer number of righteous people, God

150

would still have saved the Land. Do not stop asking and pleading; let the final decision be God's.

For your sake, GOD will intervene.

WHEN ALL THE PEOPLE

When all the people were being baptized, Jesus was baptized too. And as he was praying, heaven was opened and the Holy Spirit descended on him in bodily form like a dove. And a voice came from heaven: "You are my Son, whom I love; with you I am well pleased." Luke 3:21-22 NIV

Jesus came to be baptized just like all the other people. But as Jesus was praying, the heaven opened. When involved like all others are, when doing things like all others are, try and put heaven's stamp on it by connecting to God in prayer.

Jesus prayed and heaven opened. The Holy spirit descended on Him in bodily form like a dove.

Involve the host of heaven, let heaven speak over you. Please, the Father, acknowledge Him always and make Him proud of you. Give Him His rightful place in your life. Amen.

WHEN PRESSED

So it was, as the multitude pressed about Him to hear the word of God, that He stood by the Lake of Gennesaret. Luke 5:1 NKJV

Jesus was pressed by the multitudes to hear the Word of God, how awesome. Yet Jesus was not rushed; He took His time to prepare His platform. He stood and looked around for a place where He would position Himself better before preaching the Word.

There were empty boats nearby, so He approached the owners. He made one of them, Simon, launch the boat away from the shore. This created some space between Him and the crowd. He then sat in the boat and preached to them.

When pressed by the crowd around us, how quick are we to respond?. Sometimes we need to take a deep breath before responding. We need to look around and prepare before launching out. Jesus could have preached straight away to the crowd, but for a more effective outreach, He needed a better platform to preach from. By sitting in the boat away from the crowd, He created a space between the crowd that helped Him reach out without the crowd pressing into Him.

When pressed in situations, look around, do not be hasty. Plan your move so as to be more effective. Do not be overwhelmed. Manage that pressed situation with wisdom.

WHO ARE YOU?

Finally they said, "Who are you? Give us an answer to take back to those who sent us. What do you say about yourself?" John replied in the words of Isaiah the prophet, "I am the voice of one calling in the wilderness, 'Make straight the way for the Lord.'" John 1:22-23 NIV

When John was asked who he was, his answer was not I am John the son of Zechariah and Elizabeth, it was not about where he came from but what he was here to do and was doing.

Yes, you are a child of God, but what are you doing?

John's answer reflected God's purpose. "I am the voice of one calling in the Wilderness, make straight the way of the Lord."

When asked who we are, what is our response? Let us ask ourselves who we are? What is your God-ordained purpose? What are you doing?

May our answer to the question put a smile on Father's face as it reflects His purpose.

WORSHIP

Then the devil, taking Him up on a high mountain, showed Him all the kingdoms of the world in a moment of time. And the devil said to Him, "All this authority I will give You, and their glory; for this has been delivered to me, and I give it to whomever I wish. Therefore, if You will worship before me, all will be Yours." Luke 4:5-7 NKJV

The fact that the devil took Jesus up the mountain to show Him the Kingdom does not make him the owner of the Kingdom. The Kingdom belongs to God, kingdom both on earth and in heaven is under God's authority.

The fact that man has taken you up and shown you the beauty that is at that high position does not give them authority over it. No matter what man has achieved, no matter their position, CEO or otherwise, they are accountable to the Supreme God. They are limited, God has positioned them but the ultimate authority, honour & power, belongs to God.

We need to remember to give God His rightful place in our lives always. If someone has shown you the way up and the beauty, you are not to turn them into a god; some would require you to worship them and might make unlawful demands from you. Worship the Lord your God and Him alone. God holds the keys that unlock high achievements. Examine what you give in to, you belong to God. You are accountable to God.

UNABLE TO RECOVER FULLY

When Shishak king of Egypt attacked Jerusalem, he carried off the treasures of the temple of the Lord and the treasures of the royal palace. He TOOK everything, including the GOLD SHIELDS Solomon had made. So King Rehoboam MADE BRONZE SHIELDS TO REPLACE THEM and assigned these to the commanders of the guard on duty at the entrance to the royal palace. 2 Chronicles 12:9-10 NIV

When the enemy attacked Jerusalem as a result of the Israelites abandoning the Lord, they stole treasures. Some treasures they stole were not recovered but replaced with something of lesser value. The GOLD SHIELDS was replaced with BRONZE SHIELDS.

When you are complacent, you give the enemy a foothold in your life and he steals from you. Some of the treasures can never be recovered or might be replaced with items of lesser value. For instance, there is time for everything and a season for every activity under the sun. If you decide to give your time to the enemy when you are meant to be engaged with profitable things, that season might be lost forever. There are consequences for entertaining the enemy.

God is merciful and is able to restore but it could cost you dearly.

Do not journey the hard way; do not let the evil lessen your benefit. Make sure you enjoy His fullness.

UNABLE TO RECOVER FULLY

When Shishak king of Egypt attacked Jerusalem, he carried off the treasures of the temple of the Lord and the treasures of the royal palace. He TOOK everything, including the GOLD SHIELDS Solomon had made. So King Rehoboam MADE BRONZE SHIELDS TO REPLACE THEM and assigned these to the commanders of the guard on duty at the entrance to the royal palace. 2 Chronicles 12:9-10 NIV

When the enemy attacked Jerusalem as a result of the Israelites abandoning the Lord, they stole treasures. Some treasures they stole were not recovered but replaced with something of lesser value. The GOLD SHIELDS was replaced with BRONZE SHIELDS.

When you are complacent, you give the enemy a foothold in your life and he steals from you. Some of the treasures can never be recovered or might be replaced with items of lesser value. For instance, there is time for everything and a season for every activity under the sun. If you decide to give your time to the enemy when you are meant to be engaged with profitable things, that season might be lost forever. There are consequences for entertaining the enemy.

God is merciful and is able to restore but it could cost you dearly.

Do not journey the hard way; do not let the evil lessen your benefit. Make sure you enjoy His fullness.

UNPOPULAR BUT RIGHT

Making the right move may be challenging and unpopular. Our choice of the decision, the move we make in life should be based on our conviction from above. Our conviction might not be acceptable by the majority, but what matters is the source of the conviction.

Being at peace with God with your conviction is all that matters. Paul saw beyond what the sailor saw; he was convinced and warned the others while sailing from Rome.

"I can see there will be a list of trouble on this trip." But the captain and the owner of the ship did not agree with Paul. Acts 27: 10-11.

The decision to keep sailing was made and based on the seen situation. "The harbor where they were was not a good place for the ship, and a good wind began to blow and they thought, "this is a good wind for them to sail," so they set off. The good wind soon turned against them; the wind turned into a storm blowing so hard. For many days, they thought they were going to die.

It was difficult to follow Paul's advice; he was just one of the prisoners on the ship. It was easier to follow the choice of the Pilot, the owner of the ship and the weather (wind) that looked good.

We are children of faith, to avoid the danger of being tossed about in life, we need to see beyond. We need to trust, believe and follow God's leadership.

UNTIE THE COLT

There is a colt that needs untying. The colt is ready to fulfil its purpose.

You did not labour for the colt, but it is now mature. It has gone through nurturing and it is now ready to be utilized. It is waiting to be untied.

Someone was employed to care for the colt. They nurtured it. It had never been ridden; it is fresh.

Jesus sent His disciples to untie a colt and bring it. "If anyone asked why you are untying it, say the Lord needs it." Luke 19:31.

The disciples went and obeyed Jesus's order. Although it was strange, untying what did not belong to them, what they did not own/labour for but they obeyed Jesus. They stepped out in boldness. When they reached the colt, they untied it and when asked why, they replied the Lord needs it. Then Jesus rode triumphantly on the colt.

There is a colt ready for you. You have not laboured for it, but God has employed someone on your behalf to care for it. Step out in boldness and it will be handed over without dispute. The colt is yours to ride on triumphantly.

"I sent you to reap what you have not worked for. Others have done the hard work and you have reaped the benefits of their labour." John 4: 38

Sometimes God is telling you to go and possess a certain thing /position but you are saying it is not yours to have. You do not feel you are entitled to it, well you are, go forth, untied it and it is yours.

When every other thing around us is suggesting otherwise, God sees the now and the future. He has given us a unique spirit (Holy Spirit) that also sees beyond. Yield to His spirit at all times. Paul's advice was UNPOPULAR BUT RIGHT.

YOU NEED TO COMPLY

What does God need to do to get your attention, how much does He need to do before you believe and follow His instructions?

God sent forth His words to you so you can act on it. So many times, we ignore it or hope that it will go away. Yes, God's instructions could be challenging to carry out, but He that instructs also makes provision for us to be able to carry it out.

His plan will not change or go away. He will do all to make sure it is fulfilled. If you refuse to comply at first, then He will instruct you again. The more He has to repeat His instruction, the more intense the consequence of not carrying it out might be. The repeated instructions are sometimes accompanied by unpleasant signs/experience as God tries to gain your consent.

The more Pharaoh refused to comply with God's instruction to let the Israelites go; the more intense and unpleasant were the experiences His people had to go through.

No need for unpleasant endurance if you listen and follow Him the very first time. Pharaoh and his people went through the unnecessary experience. God won in the end; Pharaoh had to comply. God will always win; you need to comply.

Printed in Great Britain
by Amazon